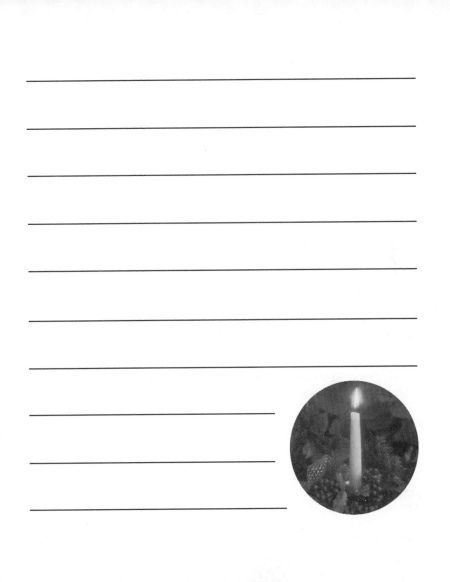

Published by Barbour Publishing, Inc., P.O. Box 719, Uhrichsville, Ohio 44683
http://www.barbourbooks.com

ecpa Member of the
Evangelical Christian
Publishers Association

Printed in China.

For unto Us
a Child Is Born

Ellyn Sanna

BARBOUR
PUBLISHING, INC.

For unto us a child is born,

unto us a son is given.

ISAIAH 9:6 KJV

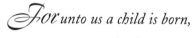 Christ Child is

the best Christmas gift of all!

Contents

At Christmastime, we celebrate the birth of Jesus of Nazareth, a Baby Who was born more than two thousand years ago. Caught up in the season's bright lights and frantic busyness, we may lose sight of the Child Whose birthday we celebrate.

But Christmas means far more than tinsel and evergreen and pretty packages. The true meaning of our celebration is this:

The Child Who was born so long ago
came because He loves you.
He wants to give Himself to you.
He was born for *you.*

A Child

*And she brought forth her firstborn son,
and wrapped him in swaddling clothes,
and laid him in a manger.*

LUKE 2:7 KJV

What a strange way for God to come to us—as a helpless, vulnerable baby! No wonder so many people alive at the time of His coming completely missed what had happened; they were expecting something far different.

God still has a way of doing that: He comes to us in unexpected ways, in small ways, in ways we may overlook if we're too busy to pay attention. But whether we notice Him or not, He is always present with us.

Look for the Christ Child's presence in your life. You may find Him where you least expect Him.

They were all looking for a king
To slay their foes, and lift them high;
Thou cam'st, a little baby thing
That made a woman cry.

GEORGE MACDONALD

Simeon and Anna were two old people who had been waiting a long time for the birth of Jesus. Those around them may have assumed they were too old to be of any use to their society. But Simeon and Anna knew what was truly most important. Their hearts were open and ready to welcome a special Child.

Simeon and Anna both conspire
The infant Saviour to proclaim;
Inward they felt the sacred fire,
And bless'd the babe and own'd his name.

Let pagan hordes blaspheme aloud,
And treat the holy child with scorn;
Our souls adore th' eternal God
Who condescended to be born.

ISAAC WATTS

Come worship the King,
That little dear thing,
Asleep on His mother's soft breast.
Ye bright stars, bow down,
Weave for Him a crown,
Christ Jesus by angels confessed.
Come, children, and peep,
But hush ye, and creep
On tiptoe to where the Babe lies;
Then whisper His name
And lo! like a flame
The glory light shines in His eyes.

Come strong men, and see
This high mystery,
Tread firm where the shepherds have trod,
And watch, 'mid the hair
Of the maiden so fair,
The five little fingers of God.
Come, old men and grey,
The star leads the way,
It halts and your wanderings cease;
Look down on His face
Then, filled with His grace,
Depart ye, God's servants, in peace.

G. A. STUDDERT KENNEDY

Unto us a Child is born!
Ne'er has earth beheld a morn,
Among all the morns of time,
Half so glorious in its prime!

Unto us a Son is given!
He has come from God's own heaven,
Bringing with Him, from above,
Holy peace and holy love.

HORATIUS BONAR

A newborn baby, the child of poor parents. . .who would have thought He could change the entire world? If you live your life as though you were the center of the world, then the life of that Baby threatens to shake your being at its very foundations. But that same Baby also offers you a greater security, a greater joy, and a greater love than any you have ever known.

I saw a stable, low and very bare,
A little child in a manger.
The oxen knew Him, had Him in their care,
To men He was a stranger.
The safety of the world was lying there,
And the world's danger.

MARY ELIZABETH COLERIDGE

Once in royal David's city
Stood a lowly cattle shed,
Where a mother laid her baby
In a manger for his bed:
Mary was that mother mild,
Jesus Christ her little child.

CECIL FRANCES ALEXANDER

Prince of Peace

And his name shall be called . . . Prince of Peace.

ISAIAH 9:6 KJV

The Christ Child's life was a present to us from God, the present of His very Self. Jesus came to our earth, bringing us eternal gifts from heaven.

One of the best of these gifts is the peace of God, the peace Jesus wants you to experience in your own life.

Peace I leave with you; my peace I give you.
I do not give to you as the world gives.
Do not let your hearts be troubled
and do not be afraid.

JESUS OF NAZARETH (FROM JOHN 14:27)

He has come! the Christ of God;
Left for us His glad abode,
Stooping from His throne of bliss,
To this darksome wilderness.

He has come! the Prince of Peace;
Come to bid our sorrows cease;
Come to scatter with His light
All the darkness of our night.

HORATIUS BONAR

What means this glory round our feet,"
The Magi mused, "more bright than morn?"
And voices chanted clear and sweet,
"Today the Prince of Peace is born!"

"What means that star," the Shepherds said,
"That brightens through the rocky glen?"
And angels, answering overhead,
Sang, "Peace on earth, good-will to men!"

JAMES RUSSELL LOWELL

King of Kings

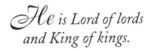

He is Lord of lords and King of kings.

REVELATION 17:14

Our world often thinks of the Christmas story as though it were a pretty fairy tale, a sentimental scene edged with sweet-faced angels, fluffy white sheep, and yellow stars. We forget that this is no Disney movie; no, this is the story that changed the world forever.

The King of creation came to live in the midst of poverty and dirt and pain—and even death. But He didn't stop being the King. His power triumphs over all earth's tragedy.

Sometimes it may seem as though the forces of evil are winning. But in reality, the Christmas Child is on His throne—and He has already won the battle.

He, the mighty King, has come!
Making this poor world His home;
Come to bear our sin's sad load—
Son of David, Son of God!

He has come Whose name of grace
Speaks deliverance to our race;
Left for us His glad abode—
Son of Mary, Son of God!

HORATIUS BONAR

The magi, those kings from the East, were wise enough to set aside their own worldly power and position. Instead, they yielded their lives to the guidance of a star—and when they found the Child, they bowed down and offered Him their treasures.

The King of glory sends his Son,
To make his entrance on this earth;
Behold the midnight bright as noon,
And heav'nly hosts declare his birth!

About the young Redeemer's head,
What wonders and what glories meet!
An unknown star arose and led
The eastern sages to his feet.

ISAAC WATTS

Bright portals of the sky,
Emboss'd with sparkling stars,
Doors of eternity,
With diamantine bars,
Your arras rich uphold,
Loose all your bolts and springs,
Ope wide your leaves of gold,
That in your roofs may come the King of kings.

WILLIAM DRUMMOND

This the month, and this the happy morn,
Wherein the Son of Heaven's eternal King,
Of wedded maid and virgin mother born,
Our great redemption from above did bring;
For so the holy sages once did sing,
That he our deadly forfeit should release,
And with his Father work us a perpetual peace.

JOHN MILTON

Joy to the world, the Lord is come!
Let earth receive her King;
Let every heart prepare him room,
And heaven and nature sing.

Joy to the earth, the Savior reigns!
Let men their songs employ;
While fields and floods, rocks, hills, and plains,
Repeat the sounding joy.

ISAAC WATTS

Hark! The herald angels sing
"Glory to the newborn King;
Peace on earth, and mercy mild,
God and sinners reconciled!"
Joyful, all ye nations rise,
Join the triumph of the skies;
With th' angelic host proclaim
Christ is born in Bethlehem.

CHARLES WESLEY

When He sent us His Son, God crossed the distance that once separated human beings from Him. Our King came to live with us. No wonder Christmas is a day of joy!

The Revelation of God

*Anyone who has seen me
has seen the Father.*

JESUS OF NAZARETH (FROM JOHN 14:9)

The Baby born in the manger was not only a helpless infant. God clothed Himself in a tiny human body—but even while Jesus was totally human, He was also totally God. We cannot understand this paradox, but somehow the Christ Child contained the Creator of the Universe. When we look at Jesus we see Who God really is—a being of love and mercy and joy.

Christ is the Word of God.
It is not in certain texts written in the New Testament,
valuable as they are; it is not in certain words which Jesus spoke,
vast as is their preciousness;
it is in the Word, which Jesus is,
that the great manifestation of God is made.

PHILLIPS BROOKS

The Revelation of God is not a book or a doctrine,
but a living Person.

EMIL BRUNNER

How can we know that what Jesus has shown us of God is the truth; or how do we know when we look into the face of Jesus that we are looking into the face of God? The answer is so plain and simple that it is a marvel how intelligent men can manage to miss it as they do. Look at what Christ has done for the soul of man: that is your answer. Christianity is just Christ—nothing more and nothing less. It is a way of life, and He is that way. It is the truth about human destiny, and He is that truth.

R. J. CAMPBELL

Nothing more wondrous in this world
ever will men's lips tell of,
God coming to us, he that created all of creation,
As God and as man, and God as a man,
Equally gifted.
Tremendous, tiny, powerful, feeble,
Cheeks fair of colour,
Wealthy and needy, Father and Brother. . . .
This, sure, is Jesus, whom we should welcome.

THE CELTIC TRADITION

The wonder of the incarnation can only be accepted with awe.
Jesus was wholly human, and Jesus was wholly divine.
This is something that has baffled philosophers
and theologians for two thousand years.
Like love, it cannot be explained, it can only be rejoiced in.

MADELEINE L'ENGLE

The Child Who Was
Born for You

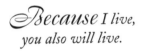 *I live,*
you also will live.

JESUS OF NAZARETH (FROM JOHN 14:19)

Christ is the source of joy. . . .
His people share His life, and therefore share its consequences,
and one of these is joy.

HENRY DRUMMOND

The Christmas Child was born long ago in a faraway land—but His birth is not irrelevant to you today. He was born for you, so that He could share God's light and life—and joy and peace—personally with you.

Savior of the nations come,
Virgin's son, make here thy home!
Marvel now, O heaven and earth,
That the Lord chose such a birth.

JOHANN SEBASTIAN BACH

Jesus came!—and came for me.
Simple words! and yet expressing
Depths of holy mystery,
Depths of wondrous love and blessing.
Holy Spirit, make me see
All His coming means for me;
Take the things of Christ, I pray,
Show them to my heart today.

FRANCES RIDLEY HAVERGAL

O *holy Child of Bethlehem,*
Descend to us, we pray,
Cast out our sins, and enter in,
Be born in us today.
We hear the Christmas angels
The great glad tidings tell;
O come to us, abide with us,
Our Lord Emmanuel.

PHILLIPS BROOKS

Given, not lent,
And not withdrawn, once sent,
This infant of mankind, this One,
Is still the little welcome Son.

New every year,
Newborn and newly dear,
He comes with tidings and a song,
The ages long, the ages long.

ALICE MEYNELL

The whole of history is incomprehensible without Jesus.

ERNEST RENAN

The second person in God, the Son, became human Himself: was born into the world as an actual man—a real man of a particular height, with hair of a particular color, speaking a particular language. . . . The eternal being, Who knows everything and who created the whole universe, became not only a man but (before that) a baby. . . .

The Son of God became a man to enable men to become sons of God.

C. S. LEWIS

O Jesus, thank you for being born for us,
God in a baby, wonderfully impossible, but true.

MADELEINE L'ENGLE

We may feel afraid to look into the Christ Child's face. But He has a message to bring us from the Father, a message of love. He says to each of us:

I have called you by name, from the very beginning.
You are mine, and I am yours.
You are my beloved, on you my favor rests. . . .
I have carved you in the palms of my hands
and hidden you in the shadow of my embrace. . . .
I never expected you would be perfect.
I love you. I love you. I love you.
Nothing will ever change that.

JAMES BRYAN SMITH

Jesus knocks at the door of our hearts, and when we open, He fills us with His joy.

CORRIE TEN BOOM

The Christ Child gives you Himself. But don't send Him away empty-handed. Give Him a gift in return—give Him yourself!

What can I give Him,
Poor as I am?
If I were a shepherd
I would bring Him a lamb—
If I were a wise man
I would do my part—
Yet what I can, I give Him,
Give my heart.

CHRISTINA ROSETTI